Scotland's Children in pictures captures the experience of being a child over the years of the twentieth century. A sample of the work of press photographers gives an authentic flavour of the joys and the hardships of children and their families — their timeless games and interests, the pleasures of high days and holidays are all here. The experience of want and war, of economic hardship and harsh living conditions are represented too, in a collection that will trigger memories for all who have ever been Scottish children.

front cover photo:
boys of Hurst Grange College skating
at Stirling, December 1937

Rudolph Kenna was born and bred in Glasgow, of Scottish–American parentage. He studied economic and social history at Strathclyde University and is the author of six previous illustrated books, with another two currently in preparation.

SCOTLAND'S children

• IN PICTURES •

rudolph kenna

in association with

First Published 1996
Argyll Publishing
Glendaruel
Argyll PA22 3AE
in association with
Caledonian Newspapers Ltd
195 Albion Street
Glasgow G1 1QP

British Library Cataloguing-in-Publication Data.
A catalogue record for this book is available from the British Library.

ISBN 1 874640 87 4

Origination Cordfall Ltd, Glasgow
Printing Cromwell Press

Scotland's Children in Pictures has been compiled from the extensive and unrivalled archive of *The Herald* and the *Evening Times*, one of the richest sources on Scottish industrial, political and social history.

Copies of most pictures in this book are available for personal or commercial use.

Contact the Photosales Department, quoting the picture reference number at

Photo Sales
Caledonian Newspapers Ltd,
195 Albion Street,
Glasgow G1 1QP

identical twins, Isobel and Elizabeth Langford, aged 3, of Motherwell have a day at Ayr beach, July 1959

Ever since amateur photography became popular in the early twentieth century, fond parents, guardians and relations have photographed children. But the pictorial record of twentieth century childhood would be greatly diminished without the contribution of press photographers and photojournalists. They used professional equipment, such as the famous Leica 35mm roll film camera, first marketed in the 1920s.

Easy to handle and fast to operate, the new generation of lightweight cameras, though initially very expensive, were ideal for candid photography, ensuring results much better than family snapshots. *Picture Post*, Britain's most famous picture magazine, first appeared in 1938, but as early as the 1920s Scotland already had *The Bulletin* and *The Bon Accord* — lavishly illustrated tabloid-style newspapers which eventually succumbed to television and now have great documentary value. By the 1950s, compact, easy-to-use cameras were ubiquitous; but family photography, as in the past, focused on happy social occasions such as christenings, birthdays and holidays and some of the most evocative and powerful images of childhood were still being captured by press photographers and photojournalists.

SC-2

yachting at Millport, July 1936

SC-3

holiday snapshot on Aberdeen beach, July 1928. The compact box camera recorded some of the most pleasurable memories of childhood

SC-4

paddling pool and sandpits in Elder Park, Glasgow, 1936

SC-5

a ride on the elephant at Edinburgh Zoo, September 1936

bathing in the ultra-modern Portobello swimming pool, July 1936 — artificial waves were among its many attractions

SC-6

The great world-wide Depression of the early 1930s was a bad time to be a child in Scotland's industrial heart. Between 1931 and 1933 more than a quarter of the country's workforce was unemployed. The bare statistic means little; George Blake captured the human tragedy in his angry novel *The Shipbuilders* (1935):

> He could not escape the significance of so many empty shops 'To Let' — newsagents, cash butchers, wireless dealers and small tobacconists: small people driven out by the sheer lack of custom. . . The workless faced him at every step: men unmistakably and irretrievably stamped with hopelessness and under-feeding, men without coats or collars, their pinched faces grey-green with cold, their hands deep in their jacket pockets, their shoulders hunched in the stoop of the damned. . . He saw men selling apples from barrows, men oscillating between mendacity and commerce with boxes of Russian matches on the pavements' edges, men selling briquettes from hired floats, and men imitating Charlie Chaplin to the music of penny-accordions.

The infamous Means Test was bitterly resented. Introduced in 1931, it came into effect when unemployed people exhausted

making mud pies in the backcourt of Florence Street in Glasgow's Gorbals — this scene reminiscent of the Depression years was photographed in February 1963

SC-7

twenty six weeks of unemployment insurance benefit. The Means Test, administered by prying local officials, assessed all family circumstances — working sons or daughters and disposable assets such as wireless sets. By applying the Means Test with inquisitorial rigour, the authorities cut down welfare expenditure. By 1932, about 50% of all benefits were means-tested. The system split families, encouraged informers and stimulated petty tyranny on the part of officialdom.

The hated 'Means Test Man' was immortalised in song:

> Ah'm no the factor nor the gas man,
> Napoleon nor Ronald Colman.
> When ye hear me rat-tat-tat upon the door,
> Have you money in the bank or money in the store?
> Ye'd better look oot or else ah'll get ye,
> Try an dodge me if ye can,
> For ah'm neither Santa Claus nor Douglas Fairbanks,
> I am the Means Test man.

the Rae family in their room and kitchen 'single end' flat in Glasgow's Gorbals — such housing was commonplace for many families in Scottish cities until well into the the 1970s

During the Depression, the abandoned hull of Ship No 534 — the future Cunarder *Queen Mary* — towered over the tenement roofs of Clydebank. First keel plates were laid in 1930, but on Clydebank's 'Black Saturday' — December 12, 1931 — work stopped and more than 3000 men were laid off. Work did not resume until February 1934.

On Saturday, March 24, 1936, shortly before the newly completed liner was manoeuvred from the fitting-out berth, thousands of youngsters enjoyed conducted tours of the *Queen Mary's* principal rooms — magnificently decorated with mural paintings and sculptured friezes by leading artists. It would be hard to imagine a more striking contrast to their own physical environment of densely packed tenements.

Enormous crowds — estimated at three quarters of a million — gathered at vantage points along both banks of the Clyde to see the *Queen Mary* go down river from John Brown's shipyard; 11,000 Greenock schoolchildren cheered as the liner arrived at the Tail o' the Bank. Special trains brought thousands of sightseers to Gourock where the great ship rode at anchor.

The excitement engendered by the occasion was more than media hype. The liner was a symbol: she proved to Scotland's people that the Depression had not extinguished Clydeside's unrivalled skills. The largest passenger vessel ever launched from a British shipyard had been built by men who had endured the dole and the Means Test. With the approach of war in the late 1930s, rearmament helped generate employment in Scotland. As the thirties drew to a menacing close, defence orders brought work to firms such as precision engineers Barr and Stroud — in 1939 the company's sales topped £1million for the first time.

Brownies waiting their turn to board the newly -completed Queen Mary *at Clydebank, March 24th, 1936*

In the summer of 1938, Scotland presented a dynamic image to the rest of the UK by staging the Empire Exhibition, which drew thirteen million paying visitors to Glasgow's Bellahouston Park. The exhibition captured the architectural spirit of the age in an exhilarating alternative Scotland of gaily coloured *art moderne* buildings set amid fountains and cascades — a utopian scene as removed from reality as Portobello from Palm Beach.

For most children the architecture of tomorrow was less interesting than Billy Butlin's sixteen acre amusement park, which cost £225,000 and boasted a hundred-foot-high scenic railway and the world's largest motor dodgem track. The Stratoplane and Brooklands Racer were attractions which reflected the contemporary obsession with futuristic travel — it was, after all, the heyday of record-breaking motor racing drivers and aviators such as Sir Malcolm Campbell who broke the world land speed record in his streamlined *Bluebird* car, and Jim Mollison, whose audacious record-breaking flights captured world headlines.

SC-10

high in the list of attractions at the Empire Exhibition in 1938 were rides on the Giant Wheel, the hundred foot high scenic railway and the Whip (above)

SC-11

the Boys' Brigade and the Royal Canadian Mounted Police join forces on the opening day of the Empire Exhibition, May 1938

Between the World Wars, Christmas was not today's market-led consumerist orgy. But department store proprietors still vied with each other in the lavishness of their Christmas toy fairs. In 1938, Tréron's famous store in Glasgow's Sauchiehall Street featured *Snow White and the Seven Dwarfs* — Walt Disney's adaptation of the fairy tale was showing in cinemas all over Scotland.

SC-12

a V.I.P. appearance during the Christmas party for children of Barr and Stroud employees, held in the firm's recreational hall at Anniesland, Glasgow, December 1936

The market for expensive toys was tiny by present-day standards. In 1936, an ultra-modern flat-roofed doll's house (with electric light) cost £2 5s — more than a week's wages for most manual workers. Dinky Toys were more affordable, with prices starting at 1d. By 1938, there were more than 300 to choose from, ranging from a scale model of the *Queen Mary* to a set of modernistic bedroom furniture. Woolworth's chain stores — opening at the rate of one a week in inter-war Britain — also offered cheap toys. The reassuring slogan was 'nothing over sixpence' ($2\frac{1}{2}$p).

Children whose fathers were in work looked forward to Christmas parties; in the spartan surroundings of factory canteens, boys and girls made reckless by an unaccustomed surfeit of soft drinks and sticky buns romped through *The Grand Old Duke of York* and queued to receive gifts from Santa Claus.

(opp.) a solemn group of youngsters in Pettigrew and Stephen's Toy Fair, Glasgow, December 1937 — selling for up to £7 15s, several weeks' wages for most parents, pedal cars were beyond the reach of the majority of children

SC-13

For less fortunate children, Christmas presents frequently consisted of stockings apparently bulging with goodies, but in reality three-quarters full of cinders. Unemployed men, using materials supplied by charities, made rudimentary toys which were distributed to needy families at Christmas. Cinema patrons, regimental associations and organisations such as the Women's Voluntary Service also made special efforts to provide Christmas treats for deprived children.

SC-14

a contrast in fortunes . . .
(above) Santa distributes gifts at the annual Christmas treat for poor children held in The Picture House, Glasgow, December 1938

(opposite) Margaret Aitken keeping a personal appointment with Santa in Patrick Thomson's Toy Fair, Edinburgh 1949

There were also privileged children, living in houses with nannies, cooks and housemaids (as late as 1939, there were still more than a million female domestic servants in Britain). For them, toy manufacturers produced marvels of miniaturisation such as Hornby's model locomotive *Princess Elizabeth*, priced at a hefty five guineas in 1937 — toys which now gladden the hearts and diminish the bank accounts of late twentieth century collectors.

The 1930s were halcyon years for the UK's toy industry, with names such as William Britains and Meccano to the fore. But toys such as model anti-aircraft guns and battery operated searchlights reflected the decade's less pleasant preoccupations — throughout Europe, bombs would soon rain down on civilians.

SC-15

Until the emergence of a money-driven consumer culture, toys were expected to last. In the late 1940s, there were Dolls' Hospitals in most cities, where broken limbs were mended and casualties who had unaccountably lost the power to say 'Mama' were miraculously restored to speech. Before the 1959 debut of Mattel's Barbie doll, modelled as a trendily-dressed teenager, girls played with plump dolls which resembled their baby brothers and sisters. With growing affluence in the 1960s, expensive toys ceased to be a luxury; new toys reflected the science-minded, consumerist *Zeitgeist*: model rocket ships and robots for boys, battery-operated kitchen appliances 'just like mother's' for girls.

If, by today's standards, the children of the 1920s and '30s had few toys, they usually had access to comics, which passed from hand to hand until they were tattered and germ-laden. D.C. Thomson's *Dandy* appeared in December 1937, followed by *The Beano* in July 1938. Generations of children enjoyed the adventures of Korky the Cat, Desperate Dan, and Lord Snooty and his Pals. Korky and Desperate Dan are still going strong, but an allegedly classless society has banished Lord Snooty from *The Beano* — even though his Pals were street urchins.

(opp.) before the throwaway society — a consultation with Jack Kay the doll doctor in the Doll's Hospital in Glasgow's Trongate, 1947

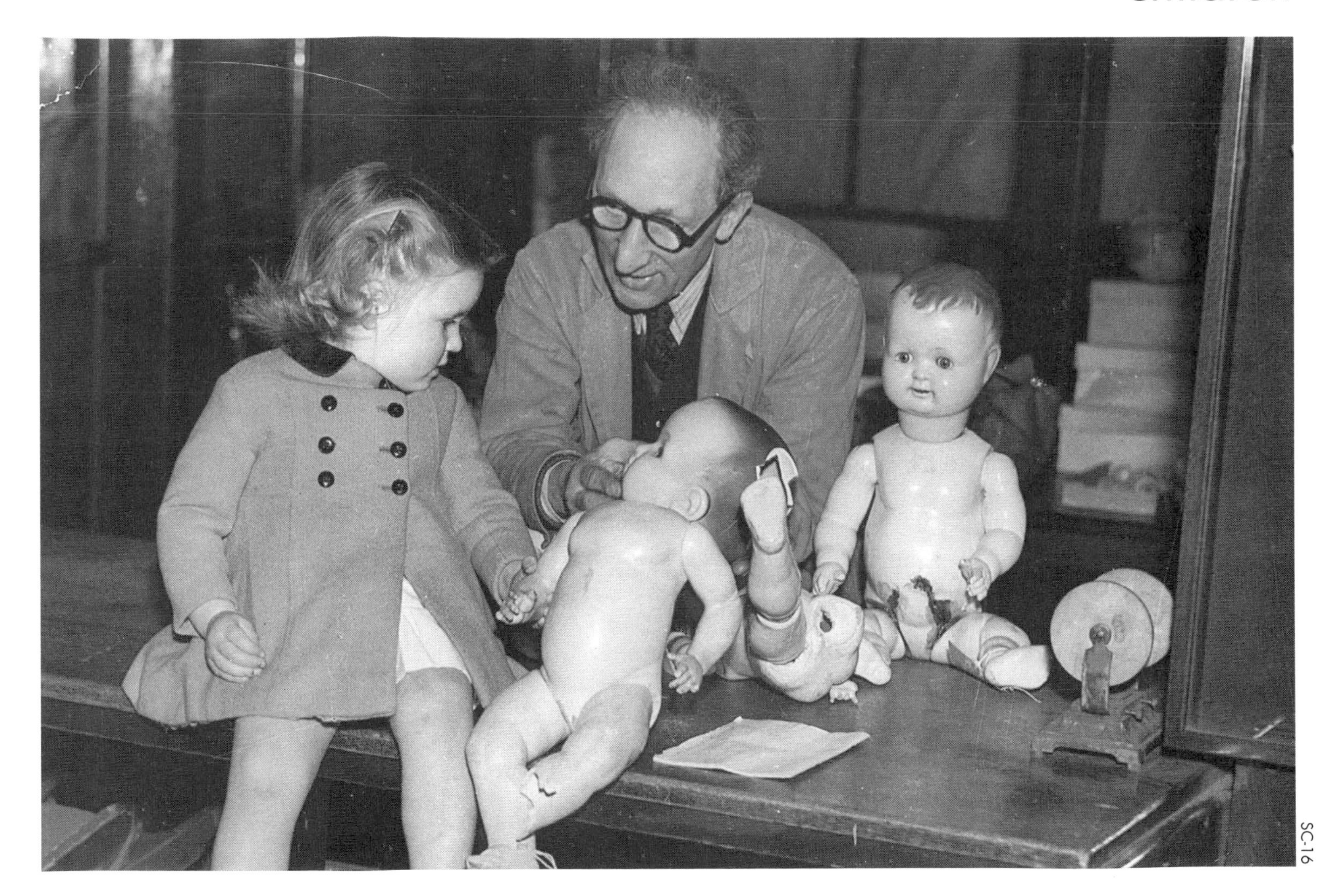

SC-16

Dundee-based D.C. Thomson also published the 'Big Five' story papers for older boys — *Rover, Wizard, Adventure, Hotspur* and *Skipper*. Early story papers for boys and girls catered for a slightly older age group than comics and leaned heavily on the strange rituals of English public schools. Small-format pulp magazines were also popular with older children. Budding detectives took hints from Sexton Blake and his trusty juvenile assistant, Tinker.

The first *Eagle* comic appeared in 1950. Interplanetary explorer Dan Dare, Pilot of the Future, became Britain's most famous strip cartoon hero. A sister paper, *Girl*, was launched in 1951. These were comics of which any parent could approve — unlike imported American crime and horror comics which, pundits believed, contributed to juvenile delinquency. The 1950s were the heyday of traditional girls' comics such as *School Friend* and *Girls' Crystal*. Contents were predictable: boarding school adventures and mystery stories set in exotic locations. The USA pioneered romantic comics for teenage girls and by the late 1950s, British publishers jumped onto the bandwagon with all-picture love story weeklies such as *Marilyn, Mirabelle, Romeo* and *Valentine*. By the mid-1960s, magazines such as *Jackie* reflected burgeoning youth culture, fuelled by teenage purchasing power.

In addition to comics there were other affordable pleasures and activities: dabbities (coloured transfers), peeries (miniature spinning tops), pea-shooters, rounders (played with balls and home-made bats), skipping ropes, yo-yos and bools (marbles). Stamps, cigarette cards and scraps were most children's introduction to the world of collectables.

Since pocket money was in short supply in inter-war Scotland, children learned to improvise. Reminiscing about his childhood in Edinburgh between the World Wars, John Webster explained:

> "If ye couldnae afford a ball, ye got a lot o newspapers and wrapped them up till they were the size of a football and ye tied it together wi a piece o string and that's what ye kicked about the street until it burst."

Team games such as Hide-and-Seek and Tig could be played without accessories. Girls spent many happy hours playing peevers (hopscotch) and skilfully stotting (bouncing) balls to rhyming chants such as "One, Two, Three, a-Leerie".

As a rule girls had less play-time than boys, since they were expected to help with housework. Howard Denton, born Howard Zoltie just before the First World War, spent his childhood in the St Leonard's Hill district of Edinburgh. He recalled:

> "The boys and girls rarely played together and I'm sure we regarded the lassies as inferior beings. A game that, strangely enough, we did have in common was the making of mud pies in the back-green. The mud was easier to work with after rain, but in the summer, when the ground was hard and dry, some of the more resourceful boys would urinate in the earth to produce a more pliable 'dough'."

In the 1920s, metal girds or hoops still found favour with many Scottish children. They were propelled along the street by a cleek (a thin metal bar with a hook or loop at the end). Children ran for miles while expertly cleeking their girds. Skates were also popular — Woolworth's stores sold them at 6d per pair in the 1930s — but few working-class youngsters possessed bicycles, though they could sometimes hire them by the hour or day, for small sums. Tommy Lang of Edinburgh remembered that:

SC-17

modern attempt at reviving the old game of cleeking your gird

old bogies never die!
Duncan Anderson of Stirling takes a life size model of himself, made at an after school project, out for a ride in his bogie

SC-18

> "They used to hire bikes out, but we were threatened 'never go on these boneshakers. They've got no brakes'. And they were dreadful things. Now they'd be arrested if they tried to put them on the streets."

(opp.) skateboarders at Maryhill
December 28, 1977

Boys made bogie carts from orange boxes and old pram wheels (a length of rope was also required for steering purposes). The steep streets of Scottish towns tested the nerves of dedicated bogie-drivers.

The play culture of Scottish children has changed considerably since the era of bogies and pavement peevers grids, but although heavy traffic has forced children's games off the streets, they are being revived in school playgrounds under adult supervision.

SC-19

Easter brought the opportunity to dye or paint hard-boiled eggs in bright colours, roll them down the nearest brae, and then eat them. Halloween was the time to don 'false face' masks, dress up in improvised fancy dress and go from house to house singing and reciting in return for apples, nuts and sweets. Now traditional Scottish 'guising' is giving way to American-style 'trick or treat'.

SC-20

savouring Easter eggs of the chocolate variety in Holyrood Park, Edinburgh, March 1959

At children's cinema matinees in the inter-war years, Friday or Saturday pennies (the usual weekly pocket money for thousands of children) bought several hours of lively entertainment. Edinburgh's Howard Denton remembered:

> "We called the Abbey our local flea-pit and I'm sure our description was pretty accurate. It wasn't unusual for me to be scratching frantically before I got back to St Leonard's Hill."

In the cinema boom years of the 1920s, all sorts of buildings were turned into rudimentary picture houses. The Glen Cinema, Paisley's oldest, was a former temperance hall. During a Hogmanay matinee on December 31, 1929, panic ensued when smoke billowed from the Glen's projection room. In the stampede

(opp.) infant pupils of Farraline School, Inverness enjoy a traditional Halloween apple-dooking ceremony, October 1938

SC-21

that followed, seventy children were crushed and trampled to death. By the mid-1930s there were plenty of purpose-built cinemas. To encourage regular Saturday attendance, cinema managers ran exciting serials ('to be continued next week') and organised children's clubs such as the Mickey Mouse Club and the Odeon Club.

If Saturday pennies were not forthcoming, then the Band of Hope offered free tea and buns and magic lantern shows — invariably with a religious or temperance message. Children as young as eight 'signed the pledge', solemnly promising 'to abstain from all intoxicating drinks as beverages'.

By 1939, nine million British families possessed wireless sets and more than a million children had enrolled in Radio Luxemburg's 'League of Ovaltineys', sponsored by the makers of the popular Ovaltine milk drink. Ovaltineys communicated by means of secret signs and mysterious code messages. The BBC's *Children's Hour* was conceived — in the words of Director-General John Reith — as "a happy alternative to the squalor of the streets and backyards". Presenters Uncle Mac (Derek McCulloch) and Auntie Cyclone (Kathleen Garscadden) received regular fan mail from

as well as Band of Hope magic lantern shows where children were encouraged to sign the pledge, seaside missions were run by the Church of Scotland, like this animated service (opposite) at North Berwick in July 1939

SC-22

young listeners, many of whom belonged to the Radio Circle, the BBC's own children's club.

Holidays away from home only became possible for less affluent people with the gradual introduction of holiday pay. The number of wage earners receiving paid holidays rose from about one and a half million in 1925 to eleven million in 1939. Until the introduction of cheap packages, holidays were taken relatively close to home. For many children in industrial west Scotland, the highlights of summer were rail excursions to resorts such as Girvan or Saltcoats on the Ayrshire coast, or trips to Loch Lomond or The Trossachs on Messrs Alexander's Bluebird motor-coaches (resplendent in Royal blue livery). Families embarked on the paddle steamers *Juno* or *Jeanie Deans* for leisurely sails to Dunoon or Rothesay. The height of self-indulgence was a full day at sea, cruising through the Kyles of Bute.

(opp.) before the era of the package tour, holidays were taken close to home — the timeless attraction of Punch and Judy on Ayr beach , June 1951

Edinburgh children had Portobello near at hand and in 1936 the resort acquired a glamorous sub-Hollywood swimming pool with heated salt water, a wave-making machine, underwater lighting, chutes, springboards and a concrete tower with five diving stages.

SC-23

During heatwaves, many city children built sand-castles in municipal parks, where sand-pits were usually provided. Those with a few pennies to spare took tram rides to outlying beauty spots; on hot summer days, Aberdeen children packed trams bound for the Links and Hazlehead Park.

A favourite holiday activity was fishing — with miniature nets on canes — for 'baggy minnows' (sticklebacks) in city boating ponds and rural burns. Caught alive, they were transported home in water-filled 'jeelie jaurs' (jam jars). Park-keepers, in spite of their reputation for enforcing regulations with draconian severity — many were old soldiers — frequently turned a blind eye to toddlers paddling in ornamental fountains. Youth movements such as the Boys' Brigade, Jewish Lads' Brigade, Boy Scouts, Girl Guides, Girls' Guildry and Woodcraft Folk organised annual camps at which many city children gained access to the countryside or seaside for the first time, while picnics and outings also took place under the auspices of the Sunday School movement.

SC-24

heatwave activity — fishing for minnows in the Water of Leith at Murrayfield, Edinburgh, July 1955

holiday boating at Largs, August 1937

SC-25

SC-26

the uniformed youth organisations provided a structure to the leisure hours of many thousands of children . . . like these Life Boys from the Dennistoun area of Glasgow in concert, February 1955

. . . and these Girl Guides from Angus taking part in a Coronation Rally at Kinnaird Castle, June 1937

SC-27

SC-28

. . . Boy Scouts having fun on the starting line of the Soap Box Derby at Glasgow Green, June 1952

in the less than affluent 1950s, much of children's recreation was organised outwith the family by Co-op societies and by employers. Saxone Welfare Association's children's sports at Kilmarnock are shown in this photo from July 1952

SC-29

Although many of the pictures in this book celebrate the red letter days of childhood, others testify to the underprivileged early environments of many Scottish children. In the inter-war period, orphanages and children's homes were frequently bleak institutions and disadvantaged children were still sent in appreciable numbers to start 'new lives' in the Dominions. Juvenile emigration was almost exclusively a phenomenon of the British Commonwealth. William Quarrier and Thomas Barnardo were both passionate advocates of the movement. The first Canada-bound Quarrier boys left Glasgow's Broomielaw in 1872.

At the beginning of this century, when the movement reached its climax, several hundred children sailed every year for Canada, Australia, New Zealand and South Africa. Canada alone received more than one hundred thousand children, many of whom were destined for lives of drudgery on isolated farms. Even in the none-too-squeamish nineteenth century, the movement aroused a degree of hostile criticism. In 1893, a *Glasgow Herald* editorial referred to "this irresponsible deportation of the unprotected". Nevertheless, it was 1967 before the last party of Barnardo children flew to Australia.

boys and girls from Quarrier's Homes, Bridge of Weir, set out for a new life in Australia, April 1939. A Glasgow Herald *editorial condemned the practice of child deportation*

SC-30

As the Second World War approached, air raid drill became part of school life. Defence authorities feared that Britain's cities would be obliterated by bombs or engulfed in poison gas in the first few days or weeks of hostilities. Forty-four million gas-masks were issued, and it was considered necessary to evacuate as many children as possible before war was declared.

The exodus of children from Scotland's designated high-risk areas — Glasgow, Clydebank, Edinburgh, Dundee and Rosyth — took place between September 1 and 3, 1939, preceded by a number of rehearsals. The Ministry of Health and the Scottish Office issued a joint statement to the effect that war was not inevitable and the evacuation scheme was purely a precautionary measure. Few people believed this disingenuous pronouncement.

In addition to gas masks, evacuees were only allowed to bring hand-luggage (for many, a brown paper parcel or carrier bag sufficed for their belongings). Ayr's Town Clerk complained that Glasgow evacuees arrived with only the clothes they stood in and claimed that foster parents had burnt the children's apparel and clothed them at their own expense.

gas mask drill in an Edinburgh school, 1939 — there were special Mickey Mouse and Donald Duck gas masks in pastel shades for younger children

On arrival at Perth, evacuees from Glasgow were taken to a school and given clothes and footwear. It was alleged that half of the Dundee evacuees received in Crieff were verminous.

The evacuation scheme was an eye-opener for Scotland's more affluent citizens, confronting them with the grim realities of urban poverty. Many were profoundly shocked by the sight of so many undernourished, ill-clothed and ill-shod children. In a letter to his wife, Prime Minister Neville Chamberlain wrote: "I never knew that such conditions existed, and I feel ashamed of having been so ignorant of my neighbours."

For many children evacuation involved long journeys on non-corridor trains devoid of toilet facilities. One train from Glasgow took twelve-and-a-half hours to reach Aberdeenshire, arriving at 12.30am on the Sunday morning on which war was declared. An Ayrshire teacher, Alec Sloan, later described the traumatic arrival of Glasgow evacuees in his home town of Kilwinning:

> "The special train had made innumerable unscheduled halts, at apparently every house by the railroad tracks and finally reached Kilwinning more than an hour and half late,

(opp.) pupils from Mathieson Street School in Glasgow's Gorbals on their way to Eglinton Street Station, September 1939 during training for evacuation — note the gas mask boxes being carried

SC-32

> at nearly one o'clock. The rolling stock was the normal third class type in current use, ten seats per compartment, non corridor and with no toilet facilities. By the time it pulled into Kilwinning Station, it was smelling to high heaven, from the engine tender at the front to the guard's van at the rear. Fully five hundred souls scrambled down on to the platform, mothers with babes in arms, aunties holding grimly to the sweating clammy palms of bewildered children, unaccompanied youngsters in every stage of mental upset in this calamity, from fear and tears to a brash acceptance of a thrilling adventure."

When actual billeting began, there was much delay and confusion. Foster parents in reception areas were frequently allowed to choose the children they wanted — and many wanted a curly-haired little girl similar to Shirley Temple, the idolised American child movie star. Those who were last to be selected never forgot the experience. Reception area hosts with large houses were often unwilling to accommodate their fair share of wartime guests.

(opp.) Glasgow children being evacuated in the aftermath of the Clydebank Blitz, April 1941 — evacuation of children from Scottish cities was an eye-opener for the country's more affluent citizens

SC-33

One report alleged, "Wealthy householders having the ear of the billeting officers selected their evacuees first, and they mostly chose unaccompanied children." On Arran, it was reported that "higher class houses got rid of the evacuees to poorer houses who willingly took them as they were getting a let at a time of year they didn't expect." In fact, many poorer householders were grateful for the billeting allowance (10s 6d for one child, or 8s 6d a week if more than one was taken), which meant useful additions to family incomes.

On reaching their various destinations, some children had good reason to be upset. Jenny Chaplin, evacuated (by grey painted Clyde steamer) from Glasgow's Govan to the Clyde coast, recalled that on arrival the evacuees were herded into a church hall; as a precaution against head lice, the boys had their heads shaved while the girls were given short pudding basin haircuts.

Not everyone took advantage of the voluntary evacuation scheme. In Dundee, only nine thousand turned up at the appointed time. In Glasgow the initial response was around 50%.; in Edinburgh only 30%. By December Britain was experiencing the 'Phoney War'; expected air raids had failed to

official propaganda described the evacuated children's idyllic existence—ecacuees prepare to 'dig for Victory' (opp.), Inverness-shire, October 1939

SC-34

materialise and of 120,000 Glasgow schoolchildren evacuated in September, more than 75% returned to the city by Christmas. But after the devastating two-night Blitz on Clydebank in March 1941 in which many young children were among the casualties, a second evacuation scheme was put into operation.

As the threat of invasion loomed in the summer of 1940, the Government set up a programme of evacuation to Canada, Australia, New Zealand and South Africa. It came to an abrupt halt in September of that year when a U-boat torpedoed the *City of Benares*. Out of ninety child 'seavacs' on board, only thirteen survived.

To bolster civilian morale, official propaganda described the evacuated children's idyllic existence, collecting wild flowers, berry-picking, rambling and doing lessons *al fresco*. Some city children did not adjust readily to rural life. Used to cinemas, cafes, fish and chip shops and free entertainment in the shape of buskers, rag and bone merchants and Salvation Army bands, they found their new environment totally alien. For others, evacuation was a positive experience which left them with a lasting appreciation of the countryside.

pulling together for the war effort — Perth children (opposite), not evacuees, run a concert in aid of the Spitfire Fund to buy aeroplanes for the RAF

SC-35

For some fortunate children, evacuation was an 'Arabian Nights' transformation. Many private schools organised their own evacuation schemes. Junior pupils of Glasgow's Laurel Bank School for Girls were accommodated in Strathallan Castle in Perthshire, where music lessons took place in the beautiful Chinese Room. Senior girls went to Auchterarder House, where paintings by Corot and Fantin-Latour hung in the drawing-room.

Children helped the war effort gathering sphagnum moss (used for hospital dressings), working in allotments in response to the Ministry of Food's exhortation to 'Dig for Victory', and holding concerts in aid of the Red Cross and the Spitfire Fund. They also participated in salvage drives, collecting waste paper, jars and bottles, scrap metal, rags and bones, and old gramophone records.

during wartime rationing conditions sweets were not available — these girls are making the most of it when sweets came off the ration in April 1949

SC-36

Dreadful living conditions in the first half of the twentieth century had adverse effects on the health and welfare of tens of thousands of children. In the 1920s, 27% of Glasgow's population lived in houses with more than three persons to a room; the corresponding statistic for Manchester and Birmingham was only 1%. For many children the only play areas close at hand were tenement back courts with open middens. Between 1919 and 1939, more than two hundred thousand council houses were built in Scotland, but demand far outstripped supply and the outbreak of the Second World War brought an end to the rehousing programme.

After the war, overcrowding was exacerbated by the 'baby boom'. In 1946, Glasgow's City Engineer estimated that it would take five to ten years to clear the city's slums and eliminate the chronic overcrowding that helped to spread the 'white plague' of pulmonary tuberculosis.

squatting in military property was the desperate response of some to the post war housing shortage — (opposite) some of the 116 children who lived in ex-army huts at Carmunnock enjoy playtime

The early post-war squatters' movement saw the peaceful occupation of empty property, including disused military and prisoner-of-war camps. By October 1946 more than forty six thousand squatters had taken possession of almost twelve

SC-37

hundred military camps throughout the British Isles. Squatters enjoyed public support; in Dundee they commandeered a large house after Polish troops moved out. In Falkirk, a crowd gathered to cheer three squatters fined 5s each under the 1865 Trespass Act. At Prestwick RAF base, squatters took over part of the camp while service personnel were enjoying themselves at a dance, and in Glasgow and Aberdeen they occupied upmarket hotels.

Although Clement Attlee's Labour Government was prepared to countenance the squatters' invasion of unused military camps, it cracked down on the movement when it appeared to threaten the stability of a property-owning society. Naming the Communist Party as the instigator and organisers of the movement, a Government statement declared: "Unless steps are taken . . . anarchy may result."

In Glasgow in 1946, women and children, including twelve expectant mothers, were unceremoniously ejected from the city's exclusive Park Circus Place. As late as 1949, having nowhere else to go, fourteen families of squatters moved into a condemned tenement in Glasgow's Shamrock Street. They stayed on, even after workmen had taken off the roof and removed all doors and windows.

forlorn-looking Morag McArthur beside her mother's furniture after being evicted from a house occupied by squatters in Glasgow's Park Circus Place, September 1946

SC-38

Initially, only a small minority qualified for stop-gap factory-made 'pre-fabs', but by the end of Labour's term in office in 1951, more than one million permanent houses had been built. Five new towns — East Kilbride, Glenrothes, Cumbernauld, Livingston and Irvine — arose in the post-war years to take overspill from the congested cities. Yet as late as 1967, a third of Scottish families were still living in inadequate accommodation, including run-down tenements where it was not unusual for four families to share a stairhead toilet.

While the media usually concentrated on the most sensational aspects of the notorious Glasgow slums, it is worth remembering that the inhabitants often did wonders with meagre resources. With the end of Austerity in the 1950s — and the more ready availability of hire-purchase — single-ends (one-apartment flats) were transformed into 'wee palaces', with modern cookers, fireplaces and furniture.

For many Scottish families, the 1950s and '60s was the time of the 'Big Flit': the long-awaited move to a brand new council house with several apartments and — most gratifying of all — a bathroom with hot water on tap.

Between the World Wars, the majority of babies were born at home, frequently in the hole-in-the-wa' bed recesses of single-ends. The pre-war Health Insurance scheme did not apply to the dependants of insured persons, and many people could not afford to pay for the professional services of a doctor. Children were dosed with patent medicines and time-honoured family remedies, including laxatives such as senna and castor oil. A salt-filled sock, tied round the neck, was the recognised 'cure' for a sore throat, while earache called for the application of a hot onion. Chest complaints were treated with hot kaolin poultices, applied front and rear and secured with tight bandages. Before 1948 the majority of hospitals in Scotland depended on voluntary contributions and medical staff were obliged to ration their pitifully inadequate resources.

In his memoirs *A Life Worth Living*, Dr W.A. Murray described the conditions in Glasgow's Victoria Infirmary in the early 1920s. Tonsillectomies were carried out on juvenile outpatients. When the tonsils had been extracted, the child was carried back to the waiting-room, where other terrified youngsters awaited their turn for the operation:

"What was surprising was that, after a short interval, mothers and children went home in a tramcar. I learned later that this was known locally as 'the sawdust car' because of the necessity of spreading sawdust to mop up the blood."

Rickets — vitamin D deficiency, leading to malformation of the bones — was still fairly common in the 1920s. Bow-legged children were a familiar sight in the poorer areas of Scottish towns. The Save the Children Fund reported more malnutrition in 1932 than in 1931, the *Annus Mirabilis* that saw a 10% cut in unemployment benefit (from 17s to 15s 3d). The Milk Act of 1934 ensured that schoolchildren got one-third of a pint of milk every day for a halfpenny, or without charge if they were receiving free meals. By 1937, only 1.5% of children suffered from rickets. The condition disappeared in the 1940s, with the regular free issue of cod liver oil, high in vitamin D.

(opp.)
twins Sheena and Elizabeth Farquhar, pupils of Kennoway School in Fife, enjoy their milk ration, December 1950 — free school milk and the slightly less popular cod liver oil were introduced to combat poor diet as evidenced by the prevalence of rickets in the 1920s and '30s

SC-39

As late as the 1930s, diseases such as diphtheria and meningitis claimed the lives of many Scottish children. In 1930 there were 4,960 cases of scarlet fever in Glasgow alone, resulting in forty one deaths. By 1954 the number of cases in the city had been reduced to 1,350 and there were no fatalities.

In 1948, when the National Health Service came into operation, seven of Glasgow Corporation's seventeen hospitals dealt with fever and tuberculosis patients. The 'fever van', which conveyed children to hospital, was still a familiar sight in many districts. Fever victims were kept in quarantine. Bedside visits were not allowed, so parents were unable to speak to their children for weeks on end, though they could communicate by signs through glass partitions. In the 1950s, mass vaccination campaigns helped eliminate scourges such as tuberculosis and polio.

In the early twentieth century, childcare was largely the responsibility of extended families, but there were pioneering nurseries, including Chessel's Court Nursery School in Edinburgh and the Phoenix Park Kindergarten in Glasgow. During the First World War, as women were recruited into industry, the Government was obliged to offer childcare facilities, but with the return of peace these facilities were withdrawn. Between the Wars, the provision of nursery classes covered barely 10% of the under-five population. With the resumption of hostilities, the State was again forced to make national arrangements for childcare. But when the Second World War ended day nursery places in Scotland were greatly reduced again.

Nancy Wyllie (left) and friends Douglas Hamilton and Wilma Carey in a Glasgow Corporation Nursery, August 1951 — this was one of the very few child care facilities in existence

SC-40

As late as the 1950s, most children were still taught in Victorian schools, erected under the provisions of the 1872 Education (Scotland) Act, which made schooling in 'the three Rs' of reading, writing and arithmetic compulsory for children up to the age of thirteen. Many of these schools had imposing stone exteriors. Internally, they were all too frequently grim and forbidding: windows were set high up so that pupils could not see out of them; walls were painted dull green or brown; heavy metal-framed desks and seats were firmly fixed in regimented rows. In his enlightened Scotland Street School (now Glasgow's Museum of Education), Charles Rennie Mackintosh showed that the stringent financial limitations of Victorian School Boards could be overcome by the imagination and humanity of a great architect.

(opp.) painting for Primary 7 pupils at Hillhead High School, Glasgow, February 1953 — even for the imaginative arts, the traditions of firm discipline, sitting in rows and working in silence are evident

SC-41

Youngsters leaving school without qualifications (up until very recent years, the vast majority) constituted a cheap labour pool and were recruited in large numbers for dead-end jobs as errand boys, packers, shop assistants and housemaids. As late as 1948, influential educationalist John Newsome argued that boys and girls should be taught differently. In practice, this meant that girls took domestic science and commercial studies such as typing and shorthand, while boys did woodwork, technical drawing and metal work (industrial Scotland was still a nation of 'metal bashers'). In the 1940s, Edinburgh Corporation Education Department ran a School for Little Housewives at Leamington Terrace. Girls went on a four week training course, during which they learned the finer points of Housewifery.

Classroom shortages became severe in 1947, when the school-leaving age was raised from fourteen to fifteen. The short-term solution was the construction of hundreds of pre-fabricated aluminium huts. Shortages of labour and materials were gradually overcome, and by the 1960s many children were being educated in modern schools with bright, well-ventilated classrooms.

an all-girl cookery class in co-educational Harris Academy, Dundee 1953 — girls were encouraged in the arts of housewifery

SC-42

Discipline was strict under the traditional Scottish education system. Many older people remember excessive use of the tawse or belt — a strip of toughened leather which, wielded with enthusiasm, inflicted painful lesions on hands and wrists. Corporal punishment was meted out to slow learners as readily as to badly behaved pupils. Individualism was strongly discouraged.

Retired mariner John Nicolson, who went to school in Torrance and Raasay in the 1930s, was left-handed. He later wrote: "Any ideas I may have harboured about writing with my left hand were soon dispelled and a few cracks on the knuckles with a ruler corrected the defect!" The authoritarian atmosphere was temporarily suspended when pupils set off in crocodile file to treats like Bertha Waddell's famous Children's Theatre, which gave performances the length and breadth of Scotland, in village halls and schools as well as in orthodox theatres.

(opp.) light relief — a section of the audience of school pupils watch a performance of Bertha Waddell's Children's Theatre in the Springburn Co-op Hall, Glasgow, December 1950

SC-43

SC-44

the value of education to compensate for disadvantage was a cherished belief — here, under the watchful eye of their teacher children play netball at Castle Toward Residential School near Dunoon in March 1951. Glasgow Corporation ran twelve such schools for convalescent and handicapped children

as well as a traditionally firm emphasis on the three Rs, schools in Scotland have always cherished the notion of providing a culturally enriching educational experience — here young members of St Patrick's School Choir seem to be enjoying their prize-winning performance in the Lanarkshire Music Festival, March 1952

SC-45

The more relaxed 1960s saw a much broader interpretation of education. In junior schools, the curriculum was widened and teaching became more child-centred. In new open-plan classrooms, children no longer had to sit in rows and were comparatively free to move about. With growing affluence, study trips became an important part of the learning process.

Irish, Italian, Russian, Lithuanian and Polish immigrant children had been a feature of Scottish life for generations. and by the 1950s children from the New Commonwealth began to arrive in Scotland. In 1950, the Asian community numbered about six hundred people. By 1970, the total population of Asians in Scotland was about 16,000 and by 1980 the community had grown to about 32,000, including Pakistanis, Indians, Chinese, Bangladeshis and Vietnamese.

The bulk of these ethnic minorities settled in the Strathclyde region, predominantly in Glasgow, where the Gorbals had a long tradition of absorbing minorities. By 1981, when the era of New Commonwealth immigration had come almost to a close, the total population of all the ethnic minority groups in Scotland was estimated at 38,400. As the education system adapted to the

SC-46

schoolchildren disembark from the Dunera *at Greenock at the end of an educational cruise to the Mediterranean, April 1961*

(opp.) early learning in multi-racial Gorbals Primary School, Glasgow, February 1957

SC-47

needs of a multi-cultural society, children of different ethnic backgrounds began to form close friendships and learn something of other cultures, beliefs and customs.

SC-48

English lesson for immigrant children at Wallace Street School, Gorbals, 1975

One of the most significant educational developments of the last decade has been the revival of interest in the Gaelic language. *Comhairle nan Sgoiltean Araich* was set up in the 1980s to establish pre-school Gaelic playgroups, and by 1992 approximately a hundred such groups were in place throughout the Highlands and Lowlands. Children from the playgroups can continue with Gaelic-based education through Primary school.

SC-49

teacher Anne MacNeil from the island of Barra with her Gaelic class in Sir John Maxwell School, Glasgow, August 1985

SC-50

carrying on the traditions — Linda Nixon (left) and Margaret Lauder perform the sword dance at the Bute Games, Rothesay, August 1959

Shirley and Simpson Moore and Connie Macrae, from Kyle of Lochalsh, arrive in Inverness for the National Mod, September 1957

SC-51

It was not until the Coronation year of 1953 that television ceased to be an unimaginable luxury and began to enter ordinary homes through the convenience of 'easy payments'. In time, television would create a blasé public, but as late as 1952, when Chipperfield's Circus arrived in Glasgow, thousands of people lined the streets; many children followed the elephants from Queen Street Station to Queen's Park Recreation Ground. In that innocent age, few people seem to have been shocked by the spectacle of performing animals, but the days of these old-style circuses were numbered.

SC-52

clowning around at the Kelvin Hall circus, Glasgow, December 1957

Until television became ubiquitous in the 1960s, children continued to look to cinema for their idols. In February 1954, more than a thousand youngsters waited at Prestwick airport for the arrival of Roy Rogers and his Palomino horse, Trigger. When American actor, Fess Parker, famous as frontier hero, Davy Crockett arrived at Renfrew airport in April 1956, there were similar scenes of youthful enthusiasm: department stores were inundated with demands for imitation racoonskin Davy Crockett hats.

(opp.) before the TV age, crowds of adults and children line Glasgow's Victoria Road as Chipperfield's Circus comes to town, June 1952

SC-53

SC-54

before television sets were in many homes, film stars drew the crowds — here the arrival of Roy Rogers and his horse, Trigger at Edinburgh's Waverley Station is greeted enthusiastically — note the standard of dress and footwear

another film star is welcomed — Fess Parker, famous as 'Davy Crockett, King of the Wild Frontier' signs autographs for young admirers at Renfrew airport, April 1956

SC-55

The experience of childhood is related to changing family circumstances and values, as well as to the standards and aspirations of society as a whole. The Second World War was a watershed. After the great upheaval of evacuation, few people in Britain were any longer unaware of the extent of abject poverty afflicting millions of families. In 1942 Sir William Beveridge identified the 'five giant evils' blocking the road to post-war national renewal: Want, Disease, Ignorance, Squalor and Idleness. After the Second World War, the punitive Poor Law vanished from the statute book. The Welfare State arrived, dedicated to a fairer and more equal United Kingdom.

Children were among the principal beneficiaries of radical social change. The majority were better clothed, fed and housed than ever before. But with the return of high levels of unemployment in the 1980s, coupled with the erosion of welfare, a growing number of Scottish families experienced rising levels of economic hardship, and the divide between the nation's most privileged and least privileged children widened. A report published by the Child Poverty Action Group in 1996 shows that a third of Britain's children are growing up in relative poverty. In 1979 the figure was one in ten.

On the eve of a new century, it appears we have still some way to go to achieve for Scotland's children the aims of the United Nations Convention on the Rights of the Child: that all children should have "a standard of living adequate for their physical, mental, spiritual, moral and social development."

walking into the future? — these boys were taking part in a trekking holiday in Lanarkshire in July 1957, when they stayed in a different school every night

SC-56

SC-57

good fun at any age —
rolling a giant snowball at Tynecastle,
Edinburgh, January 1937

SC-58

thank you and good-bye—
these children were enjoying the King's Birthday holiday on Glasgow's Hogganfield Loch, 22nd May 1937

back cover pictures:

(top) *lunch break at the Salvation Army musical holiday camp at Dounan's Camp, Aberfoyle 1949*

(middle, left) *children of the nineties share the excitement of a gird*

(middle, right) *a spirited snowball fight in Johnstone, Renfrewshire, during 1947. The winter of 1946/47 was one of the most severe for three-quarters of a century.*

(bottom, left) *enjoying the Scottish Exhibition Centre Carnival, Glasgow 1986*

(bottom, centre) *Rutherglen children greet King and Queen with a fling of patriotic bunting, May 1938*

(bottom, right) Cynthia Hamilton and her collie Laddie at the RSSPCA Dog Show, Edinburgh 1949